Hindu Festival Tales

written by

Kerena Marchant

illustrated by

Rebecca Gryspeerdt

HODDER
Wayland

An imprint of Hodder Children's Books

Festival Tales

Christian Festival Tales • Hindu Festival Tales
Jewish Festival Tales • Muslim Festival Tales

© 2000 White-Thomson Publishing Ltd

Produced for Hodder Wayland by
White-Thomson Publishing Ltd
2/3 St Andrew's Place
Lewes BN7 1UP

Series Concept: Saviour Pirotta/Philippa Smith/Polly Goodman
Editor: Margot Richardson
Designer: Jane Hawkins
Consultant: Rasamandala Das
Music score: John Nicholson

Published in Great Britain by Hodder Wayland, an imprint of Hodder Children's Books

The right of Kerena Marchant to be identified as the author and Rebecca Gryspeerdt as the illustrator
of this Work has been asserted by them in accordance with
the Copyright, Designs and Patents Act 1988.

A catalogue record for this book is available from the British Library.

ISBN 0 7502 25947

Printed and bound by EuroGrafica, Vicenza, Italy.

Hodder Children's Books
A division of Hodder Headline Limited
338 Euston Road, London NW1 3BH

Contents

Prahlad and the Demon

Holi is the joyous Spring festival. It celebrates new life and the triumph of good over evil. Traditional Holi stories are about one of the most important Hindu gods, called Vishnu. Many Hindus consider Vishnu to be the supreme god (God himself) who, from time to time, comes down to save the world from evil.
At Holi, bonfires are lit to remember events from this story.

A long time ago, the world was ruled by an evil demon. Like all demons, he was the enemy of the gods. He was cruel and he liked to torture and kill people. Everybody lived in terror of the demon and they prayed to the gods to save them.

The gods could do nothing to help because it was impossible to kill the demon. He lived under a spell of protection that said he could not be killed by a god, a human or an animal. There was no place on land or in the sky, indoors or out of doors that he could be killed. He could not be killed during the day nor during the night. He could not be killed by any weapon.

The demon's cruelty increased and soon the whole of creation cried out to Vishnu to save them. Time after time, Vishnu had come to save the world from evil and now his help was needed more than ever before.

Prahlad, the demon's son, had given up his father's evil ways and become a follower of Vishnu. When the demon found out that his son followed Vishnu, his anger was so great he decided to kill Prahlad.

The demon threw Prahlad into a pit full of snakes. Some were poisonous and could kill him with a deadly bite, and some could crush him to death. Whichever snake killed him, it would be painful! The demon watched with glee to see Prahlad die.

Prahlad prayed to Vishnu to protect him. The snakes slept and Prahlad was unharmed.

Soon the demon lost patience. 'He will die!' he cried.

Prahlad was pulled out of the snake pit and tied down on the ground. A herd of elephants were brought to trample over him. The demon watched, expecting to hear every bone in Prahlad's body break. Once again, Prahlad prayed to Vishnu and his prayers were answered. The elephants refused to move.

'Next time you WILL die!' the demon vowed.

A huge bonfire was lit and, as soon as the flames were hot, the demon ordered his sister, Holika, to carry Prahlad into the flames. Holika had magical powers and could not be harmed by the flames, but Prahlad would be burned to death.

Prahlad prayed to Vishnu. As Prahlad and Holika walked into the flames, neither of them appeared to burn. Suddenly, Holika went up in flames. Vishnu had destroyed her magical powers. Prahlad remained under Vishnu's protection, and walked out of the bonfire alive.

6

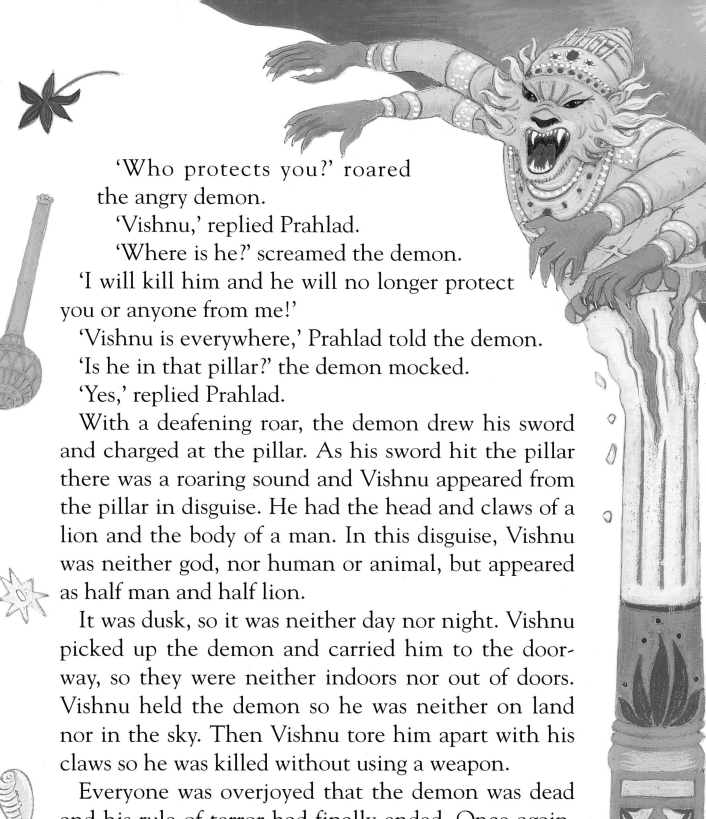

'Who protects you?' roared the angry demon.

'Vishnu,' replied Prahlad.

'Where is he?' screamed the demon. 'I will kill him and he will no longer protect you or anyone from me!'

'Vishnu is everywhere,' Prahlad told the demon.

'Is he in that pillar?' the demon mocked.

'Yes,' replied Prahlad.

With a deafening roar, the demon drew his sword and charged at the pillar. As his sword hit the pillar there was a roaring sound and Vishnu appeared from the pillar in disguise. He had the head and claws of a lion and the body of a man. In this disguise, Vishnu was neither god, nor human or animal, but appeared as half man and half lion.

It was dusk, so it was neither day nor night. Vishnu picked up the demon and carried him to the door-way, so they were neither indoors nor out of doors. Vishnu held the demon so he was neither on land nor in the sky. Then Vishnu tore him apart with his claws so he was killed without using a weapon.

Everyone was overjoyed that the demon was dead and his rule of terror had finally ended. Once again, Vishnu had saved the earth from evil, and good had triumphed over evil.

❋ Raksha Bandhan

This is a festival for brothers and sisters. They promise to protect each other, and girls and women give rakhis to their brothers, and sweets are exchanged. This poem is from a greetings card that a sister would send her brother.

On this Raksha Bandhan Day
I send you a Rakhi, and firmly pray:
May the glowing Rakhi,
Which adorns your wrist today,
Light your heart with joy and hope
And with love that's strong and true
May it brighten all your days,
Bringing health and strength to you.
God bless you, my dear brother.

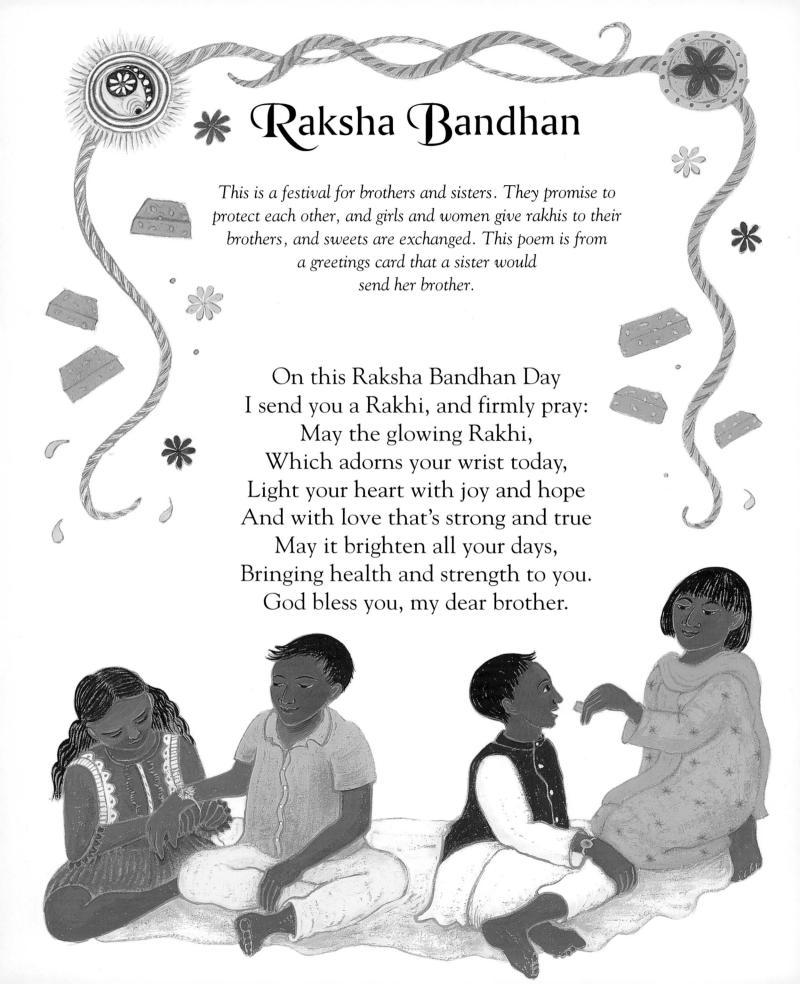

Sohan Halva

*Sweets are given to everybody as presents during festivals
and Raksha Bandhan is no exception.*

25 g cornflour

50 g sugar

250 ml water

2.5 ml (½ tsp) food colouring (your favourite colour)

2.5 ml (½ tsp) ground green cardamom

3 tbsp ghee (or margarine)

12 blanched almonds, cut in half

12 cashew nuts, cut in half

12 pistachio nuts, chopped

1 Dissolve the cornflour, sugar and water in a heavy-bottomed saucepan and place over a medium heat. Stir until the mixture becomes thick and transparent.
2 Add the food colouring, ground green cardamom, ghee, chopped almonds, cashew nuts and pistachios.
3 Continue to stir the mixture until it comes away from the bottom of the pan. When you can drop some mixture from a spoon and it falls in a lump, it is ready.
4 Remove from the heat and spread the mixture into a greased swiss roll tin or baking dish, so it is 2.5 cm thick.
5 Leave the mixture to set for 3 to 4 hours. When it has set, cut into 2.5 cm squares.

Warning
Do not cook the sweet mixture without an adult's help.
It will get very hot and could burn you.

Krishna Steals the Butter

*The festival of Janmashtami celebrates the birth of Krishna.
This is a story about the time when the God, Vishnu,
lived on earth as Krishna, in order to save the world
from another demon.*

When Krishna was born, his uncle, the wicked demon king, wanted to kill the baby. It had been foretold that Krishna would kill him one day. To save Krishna's life, his father smuggled him away to live in a faraway village among some cowherds. There, Krishna lived with his foster mother, Yasoda, and foster father, Nanda. Throughout the God's childhood, he was always getting into mischief. His foster parents, who did not know he was Vishnu, just thought he was a naughty little boy.

Every day, the women in Krishna's village would milk their cows and use the milk to make butter or yoghurt in clay pots. Krishna loved butter. It was his favourite food and he would do anything to eat it. Every day, he would put his hand in the butter pot and eat some butter, and each day he would eat more and more. Eventually, Yasoda had to hide the butter pots to stop Krishna eating all the butter. Yet this did not deter the butter thief. Krishna usually found the hidden pots, and, if he didn't, he stole butter from the neighbours' butter pots.

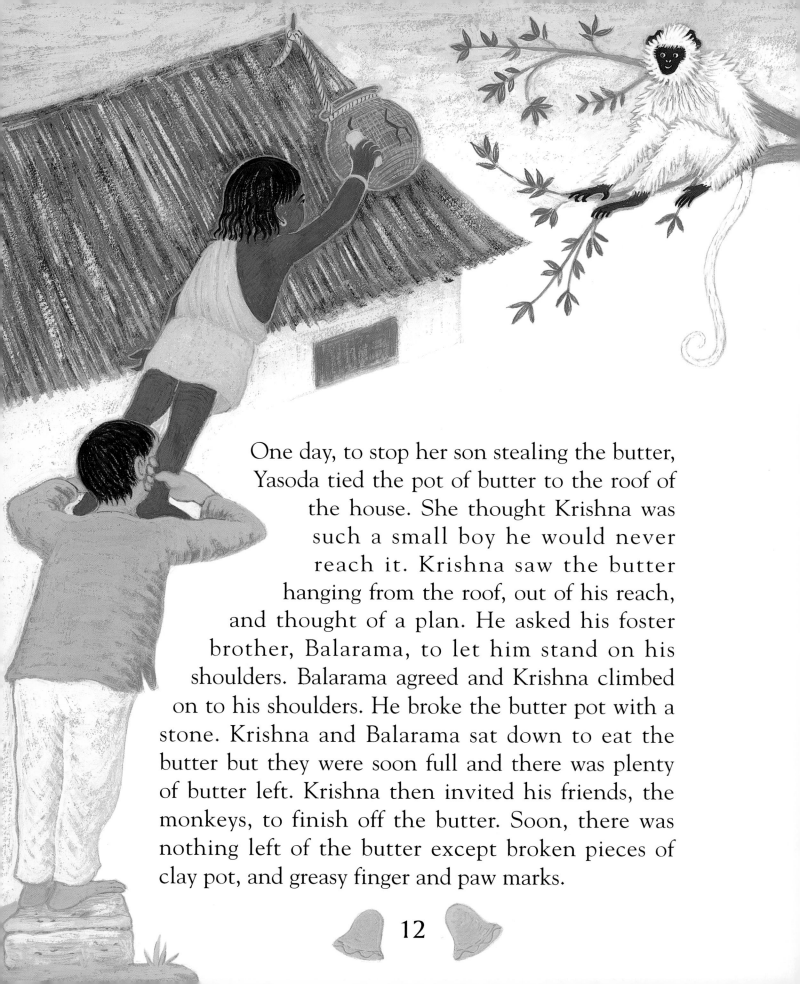

One day, to stop her son stealing the butter, Yasoda tied the pot of butter to the roof of the house. She thought Krishna was such a small boy he would never reach it. Krishna saw the butter hanging from the roof, out of his reach, and thought of a plan. He asked his foster brother, Balarama, to let him stand on his shoulders. Balarama agreed and Krishna climbed on to his shoulders. He broke the butter pot with a stone. Krishna and Balarama sat down to eat the butter but they were soon full and there was plenty of butter left. Krishna then invited his friends, the monkeys, to finish off the butter. Soon, there was nothing left of the butter except broken pieces of clay pot, and greasy finger and paw marks.

When Yasoda saw that the butter had gone and the mess the thieves had made she was angry. She chased after Krishna, determined to punish him. Krishna thought this was fun and ran round and round. Yasoda ran after him, round and round the village until, at last, she caught him.

'I'm going to punish you!' she warned. 'I'm going to tie you up. That will keep you out of trouble for a little while!'

She fetched the rope that she had used to tie the butter pot from the roof and tried to tie it round Krishna. It was not long enough to go round him. Puzzled, she fetched another piece of rope and tied it to the first rope, but it still would not go round Krishna. She brought some more rope but still it would not go round him. Soon she had used all the rope in the house and she still could not get enough to tie up a small child.

13

Eventually, it all became too much for Yasoda. Frustrated and exhausted, she burst into tears.

Krishna felt sorry for her. 'It's not your fault that you can't tie me up,' he told his mother. 'I love you, and I know how much you love me, so I will let you punish me. Go on, tie the rope round me.' Yasoda gave it one last try and the rope easily tied up Krishna, with yards and yards to spare.

Poor Yasoda. She did not know that her child was God Himself, and that no one can tie him up, even with all the rope in the world. Krishna was not actually tied by the rope, but by the pure love of his mother.

14

Ganesh Chaturthi

*This festival honours the elephant-headed god, Ganesh.
Hindus pray to Ganesh, who is the god of obstacles,
at the beginning of any important event or religious meeting.*

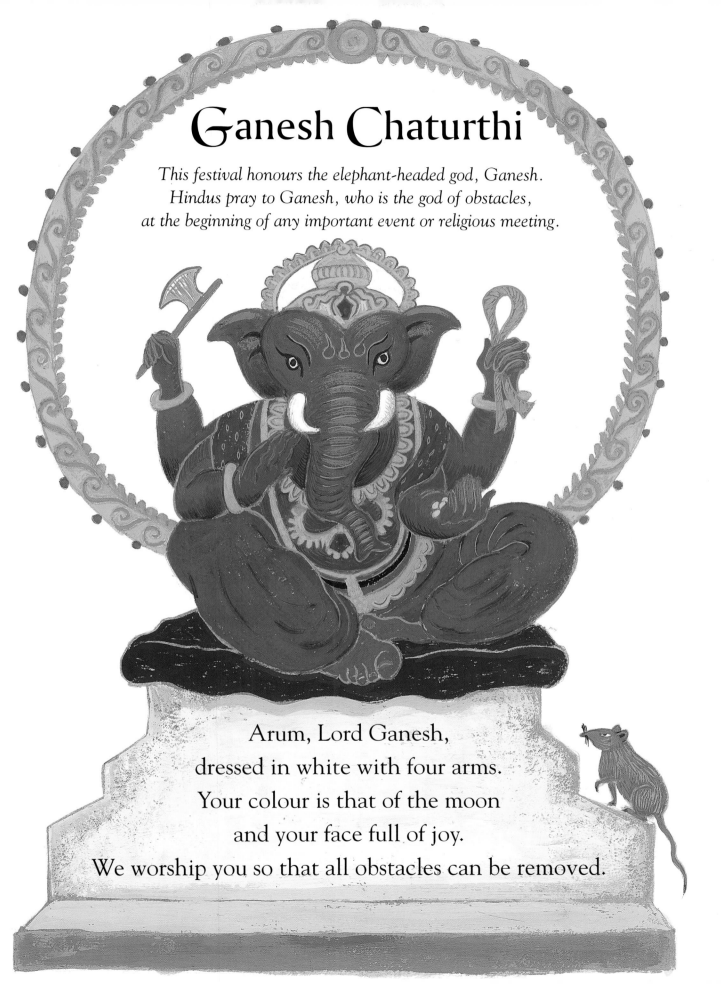

Arum, Lord Ganesh,
dressed in white with four arms.
Your colour is that of the moon
and your face full of joy.
We worship you so that all obstacles can be removed.

The Ramayana

*Dassehra is a festival that celebrates the triumph of good over evil.
During Dassehra, groups of players and dancers tour India enacting
plays from the epic poem, the Ramayana.
These plays are mimes or dances with lavish costumes and masks.
You can perform this play using dance or mime, or a mixture of both.*

Cast of characters

Four narrators   Monkeys
Prince Rama   Ravana, the demon
Sita (Rama's wife)   A golden deer
Lakshmana (Rama's brother)   An army of demons
Hanuman, the monkey general

Props

Bows and arrows for Rama and Lakshmana
Sita's jewellery   A blue sheet, to represent the sea
Orange/yellow/red crêpe-paper streamers, for fire
Cardboard swords for monkey army
Masks or face paint for the characters
Indian music for dances/background music (optional)
Cymbals

Narrator 1: Ladies and gentlemen, let me introduce our hero, Prince Rama, banished from his royal palace to live in this forest. Rama is no ordinary prince. He is God himself come to live on earth in human form as Rama.

Narrator 2: Rama did not live alone in the forest. His wife, Sita, and brother, Lakshmana, chose to share his exile.

Rama runs on with his bow and arrow, hunting in the forest. Lakshmana runs after Rama, hunting. Sita waves to them.

Narrator 3: Rama, Lakshmana and Sita were happy living in the forest. Until, one day …

Clash of cymbals. The demon, Ravana, comes on, hiding behind trees and watching Sita.

Narrator 4: The evil demon, Ravana, saw Sita in the forest. He thought she was very beautiful and he wanted her for one of his many wives.

Clash of cymbals. Ravana waves his hands, casting a spell, and a golden deer comes on. Sita tries to get it to come to her, but it runs off. Rama and Lakshmana see it. Sita points at it, and the two brothers give chase to the deer. Sita is alone on the stage.

Narrator 1: Ravana cast a spell and a golden deer appeared. Sita wanted the deer for a pet, and Rama and Lakshmana ran off to catch it for her.

Narrator 2: Sita was alone… at the mercy of Ravana.

Narrator 3: Ravana cast a spell to make Sita follow him. She tried to stay, but the spell was too strong for her and she had to follow him.

Sita sees the demon. She puts up her hands to resist him and turns her face away. Then, she slowly turns towards the demon and, step by step, approaches him. Ravana beckons her forwards and onwards, off stage. Every few steps, she drops a piece of jewellery.

Narrator 4: Every few steps, Sita dropped a piece of jewellery so that Rama and Lakshmana could see where she had gone, and find her.

As Sita leaves the stage, Rama and Lakshmana come on from another direction. They are exhausted after a long hunt.

Narrator 1: Rama and Lakshmana couldn't catch the deer, and realised that they had been tricked. They returned from their hunt. Then they stopped. Where was Sita?

Rama and Lakshmana look for Sita everywhere. They become more and more worried. Finally, they realise she has gone. Rama looks very upset and Lakshmana comforts him. A clash of cymbals. Hanuman, the monkey general, and his army of monkeys enter and kneel before Rama.

Narrator 2: Hanuman, the monkey general, vowed to help Rama find Sita.

Hanuman divides his army into groups of four and sends them off, group by group, to search for Sita. The first three groups go off stage, in different directions, and come back, sadly shaking their heads.

Narrator 3: Hanuman sent his monkeys to search for Sita. One group went north. They searched every-where, but couldn't find her.

Narrator 4: One group went west. They searched and searched, but could not find her.

Narrator 1: Another group went east. They looked everywhere but Sita was nowhere to be seen.

Narrator 2: The last search party went south. As they went, they found pieces of jewellery. They picked these up until they finally reached the tip of India and the sea.

19

The fourth group goes off in a different direction. Narrators 3 and 4 walk onto the stage with a blue sheet which they wave on the ground to represent the sea. The search party looks over the water.

Narrator 1: Over the sea lay the island of Lanka, where Ravana lived. Could Sita be there?

The search-party monkeys run back to Rama, carrying the jewellery. Rama recognises the jewellery as Sita's. The monkeys point to the south. Hanuman kneels before Rama, then sets off in the same direction. All the other characters leave the stage.

Narrator 2: Hanuman decided to see if Sita was imprisoned on the island of Lanka.

Scene 2: Ravana's palace on the island of Lanka. There are demons guarding the palace. Sita sits alone, looking unhappy.

Narrator 3: Here, in Ravana's palace on the island of Lanka, is Sita.

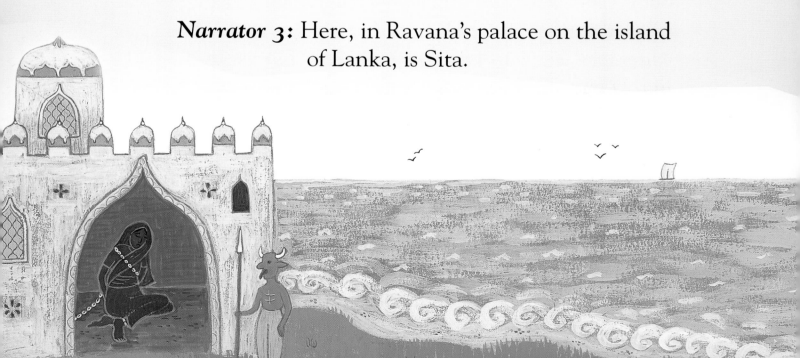

Narrator 4: Sita hopes that Rama will find her before Ravana forces her to marry him. Shhh! I can hear something!

Hanuman creeps on the stage and slips round the guards. He kneels before Sita. She is very pleased to see him. Suddenly, one of the demons sees them and, after a chase, Hanuman is captured. Ravana walks on to deal with his prisoner.

Narrator 1: Ravana ordered his demons to set fire to Hanuman's tail.

A demon guard sticks the fire streamers to Hanuman's tail. Hanuman jumps in the air and waves his tail around.

Narrator 2: Fire! Fire! Hanuman has set the palace on fire!

Some demons run off and come back with streamers, which they wave in the air. Other demons run off and return with buckets which they use to put out the fire. Hanuman stops, looks at the panic, coolly blows out the fire on his tail and escapes.

21

Narrator 3: Hanuman returned to Rama. Now that Rama knew that Sita was a prisoner on Lanka, he was determined to rescue her. A huge army gathered to fight the demon army and rescue Sita.

Rama, Lakshmana and Hanuman lead the monkey army towards Ravana and his demon army. The monkeys have cardboard swords, while the demons wave their arms, casting spells. The monkeys, led by Hanuman, bravely advance towards the demons, and touch them with their cardboard swords. To each side of the monkey army, Rama and Lakshmana fight demons with their bows and arrows.

Soon all the demons fall dead, except for Ravana. Rama then moves towards Ravana with his bow and arrow ready. They circle each other. Suddenly, Rama aims his bow and arrow at Ravana's heart. Ravana clutches his chest and falls down dead. Everybody cheers.

Hanuman leads Sita to Rama. Rama and Sita embrace.

Narrator 4: Ravana, the evil demon is dead. Sita is rescued. Good has triumphed over evil!

22

Hare Krishna

Many Hindu festivals celebrate the God Vishnu's triumphs over evil, especially when he came down to earth in human form as Krishna and Rama. This song is called a bhajan and honours Krishna and Rama. A bhajan is sung by the worshippers singing the words after the leader. Each time the song is sung, it gets faster and faster.

1. Ha - re Krish - na_____ Ha - re Krish - na_____
2. Ha - re Ra - ma_____ Ha - re Ra - ma_____

_____ Krish-na Krish - na_____ Ha-re ha - re._____
_____ Ra - ma Ra - ma_____ Ha-re ha - re._____

How Sumana Sang for the Goddess Lakshmi

Divali is the festival of lights. It is a time when Hindus hope that Goddess Lakshmi, the wife of Vishnu, will visit their homes and bring good fortune for the next year. The best Divali celebrations take place in the southern Indian province of Andra Pradesh. There, villagers erect platforms and sing songs to welcome Goddess Lakshmi.

In a village in Andra Pradesh, there lived a poor farmer called Deepak and his wife, Sumana. Deepak and Sumana were the poorest people in the village. Their small house was at the edge of the village where the soil was poor. It was all they could do to grow their vegetables. When Deepak took the vegetables to market, they were always the last to be sold at the cheapest prices as they were so small and mean compared to all the others.

Deepak and Sumana loved each other and were happy, despite being so poor. They both wanted a child more than anything else, but, despite their frequent prayers, God did not give them a child. But they were fortunate in one way: Sumana had the most beautiful singing voice in the village and whenever she sang, people would stop their work to listen. During the evenings, the village would gather round a fire to hear her sing.

The festival of Divali was approaching and everybody in the village was busy getting ready. Because Goddess Lakshmi might visit their homes at Divali, houses had to be cleaned from top to bottom and clay lamps, called diwas, had to be made. The lamps were so the Goddess could see them at night and pay a visit. Many people baked sweets and, outside their houses, drew brightly coloured rangoli patterns made of coloured rice flour.

 25

Deepak watched Sumana clean the house. He was sad because, year after year, they cleaned the house but the Goddess never visited. He wondered if it was because they didn't pray enough or because they were on the edge of the village. Or was it because they were too poor to bake sweets for the Goddess and attract her attention with bright rangoli patterns?

Just then, Deepak heard Sumana sing as she went about her cleaning. Even though he heard her sing every day, he was still surprised at the beauty of her voice. Suddenly, he had an idea. He went outside and gathered up some wood that was lying around. He began to make a platform outside the house.

Sumana heard Deepak. When she saw what he was doing, she was horrified. 'Don't make a mess,' she pleaded. 'The Goddess will never visit us if the house is untidy.'

'Don't worry,' Deepak reassured her. 'The Goddess is going to get such a welcome she will not pass by.'

Sumana was puzzled, but she trusted her husband. Why was he making a platform and why was he making torches to go round the platform?

That night was Divali night and Sumana and Deepak went without their tiny meal of rice. Instead, they placed their meal on Lakshmi's altar in their house. They said their prayers and Sumana lit the diwa to guide the Goddess to their house.

Deepak then took his wife by the hand and led her outside the house. He lifted her on to the platform and lit the flaming torches around her. 'Sing, Sumana?' he asked. 'Sing songs of welcome and praise to the Goddess Lakshmi. When she hears your voice and learns of our devotion she will not pass by our house tonight.' Sumana stood on the platform and sung into the dark night. Beside her, Deepak prayed to the Goddess.

That night, the Goddess visited houses all over India. Eventually, she came to Andra Pradesh and the lights in the houses guided her to Deepak and Sumana's village. Everybody in the village slept except for Deepak and Sumana. As the Goddess came near the village, she heard the most beautiful voice singing songs of praise and devotion to her. The Goddess turned towards the sound of the singing and let it guide her towards Deepak and Sumana's house. There, she saw Sumana singing on the platform surrounded by torches and saw Deepak praying beside her.

'Why have I never visited this house before?' the Goddess wondered. 'This couple show such devotion. They have stayed awake all night to welcome me in such a beautiful way.' Without being seen, the Goddess entered the house to bring good fortune to Deepak and Sumana.

The year that followed was a good year for Deepak and Sumana. Their greatest wish was granted, and Sumana gave birth to a son. Their fortunes also improved as their vegetables grew better and fetched higher prices.

The next year at Divali, the couple wanted to thank the Goddess for the good fortune she had sent them. Again, they built the platform and Sumana sang throughout the cold, dark night to thank the Goddess. The Goddess visited them once more to hear Sumana sing.

In the years that followed, all the other villagers built platforms and sang throughout Divali night to welcome the Goddess. But nobody sang with more beauty and devotion than Sumana.

Phalguna Holi

Festival Information

There are countless Hindu festivals that honour the different Hindu gods.
Festivals can take place at different times all over India and can vary from place
to place. The Hindu calendar is a lunar calendar consisting of 12 lunar months.
As the months are dependent on the appearance and disappearance of the moon,
the dates of festivals in the Western calendar vary from year to year.

NEW YEAR FESTIVALS   These mark the start of the Hindu calendar and are meant to bring good luck. The new year is celebrated in a variety of festivals in different areas of India.

RAMNAVAMI   Falls about a week after new year's day and celebrates the birth of Rama.

RATHA YATRA   The chariot or juggernaut festival that worships Krishna as Jagannatha or 'Lord of the Universe'. In India, huge chariots with a statue of Krishna are pulled through towns.

RAKSHA BANDHAN   A special festival for brothers and sisters. 'Raksha' means protection and 'bandhan' means to tie. During the festival, sisters tie a bracelet, called a rakhi, round their brothers' wrists and promise to protect them. In return, brothers promise to protect their sisters. Prayers are said, and gifts of sweets are made.

JANMASHTAMI   Celebrates the birth of Krishna. Pilgrims go to Vrindavan, where Krishna was born. At midnight, the hour of his birth, temple bells ring and a statue of Krishna is put into a beautiful cradle. Pilgrims rock the cradle and pray that Krishna will help them. People tell stories of Krishna; a favourite is the story of how Krishna stole the butter. Groups of boys will enact this story by standing on each other's shoulders to steal pots of milk and rice from high windows.

GANESH CHATURTHI   A festival that honours the elephant-headed god, Ganesh. There are temples of Ganesh all over India and in every hotel there is a shrine to this god of travellers. This festival is celebrated throughout India.

DASSEHRA   A nine-day festival that celebrates the triumph of good over evil. During Dassehra, groups of players and dancers tour India enacting plays from the epic poem, the *Ramayana*, which tells the story of how the God, Vishnu, came to live on earth as Prince Rama and how Rama slew the demon Ravana who abducted his wife, Sita. These plays are mimes or dances with lavish costumes and masks. Hindu cultural societies are always happy to advise schools who want to put on a performance of the Ramayana and may be able to send Indian dancers to a school. Many books on Hinduism have instructions on how to make masks. The festivities of Dassehra fall a month before the festival of Divali.

DIVALI   The festival of light. It is a time when Hindus hope for prosperity in the year to come and hope that the Goddess Lakshmi, the wife of Vishnu, will visit their homes and bring them good fortune for the next year. All over the Hindu world, the streets are lined with lights; oil lamps and candles are lit at windows; and outside houses people make brightly coloured rangoli patterns on the ground. All these efforts are to persuade the Goddess to visit the home.

MAHA SHIVA RATRI   A festival that celebrates the birth of Shiva, the Lord of Creation.

HOLI   The joyous Spring festival. All over India, bonfires are lit and everybody throws coloured paint at each other. This is a festival that celebrates new life and the triumph of good over evil. The traditional Holi stories are about the God, Vishnu, who, from time to time, would come down to earth to save the world from evil.

Magha Maha Shiva Ratri

Glossary

Bhajan A song that is sung by worshippers. A leader first sings the words and the other worshippers repeat them.

Cowherds People who look after a small number of cows.

Demon A cruel, evil person: someone who is against God.

Diwa A clay lamp that is filled with oil and lit, especially at Divali.

Evil Bad, harmful.

Exile When a person is sent away from his or her home or country.

Foretold Told of something before it took place.

Ganesh The elephant-headed god who removes obstacles from the path of religious life.

Glee Delight

Halva An Indian sweet that is like fudge.

Incarnation A form of God when He descends from His kingdom to this world.

Krishna An incarnation of the God Vishnu.

Lakshmi The wife of Vishnu. She is the Goddess of Fortune.

Lanka The old Indian name for the island of Sri Lanka. The demon Ravana lived in a fortress on Lanka.

Platform A raised, level surface (for example, a railway-station platform).

Prayed Talked to God, to ask things, or to say thank you. Sometimes, people pray silently, without saying anything out loud.

Rakhi A special bracelet given by sisters to their brothers to protect them. Rakhi means protection.

Rama One of the incarnations of Vishnu, who appeared as an Indian prince.

Ramayana An epic poem about Prince Rama.

Rangoli patterns Patterns of traditional Hindu symbols or flowers made from rice flour. These patterns are drawn outside houses at Divali.

Spell A saying or some words used as a magical charm.

Torture Make someone suffer lots of pain, as a punishment.

Vishnu One of the most popular Hindu gods. He is the protector of the world and is often considered God Himself.

Weapon A thing used to harm someone or something, such as a sword, a spear, a knife or a gun.

Index

Resources

Books

Hinduism by Katherine Prior and Dilip Kadodwala (Franklin Watts, 1995)

Celebrate Hindu Festivals by Dilip Kadodwala and Paul Gateshill (Heinemann, 1995)

Holi by Dilip Kadodwala (Evans Brothers, 1997)

Festivals: Diwali by Kerena Marchant (Wayland, 1999)

Hindu Mandir by Anita Ganeri (A & C Black, 1998)

Hindu Scriptures by V.P. Kanitkar (Heinemann, 1994)

Rama, The Heroic Prince by Michelle Esclapex (Moonlight Publishing, 1997)

Let's Celebrate; Festival Poems by John Foster (OUP, 1997)

Web sites

http://www.hindunet.org
  The Hindu Universe: features a Hindu calendar, a glossary of terms and information on Hindu arts, customs and worship.

http://india.indiagov.org/culture/religion/hinduism.htm
  Hinduism: An Eclectic ReligiousTradition. Maintained by the Indian government; gives information on Hindu beliefs and festivals.

http://www.iskcon.org.uk/ies/ – See Iskcon, right.

Other Media Resources

BBC Education produces schools programmes, videos and resource packs on different faiths, including 'Pathways of Belief'. BBC Information, PO Box 1116, Belfast BT2 7AJ
Tel: 08700 100 222
email: info@bbc.co.uk   www.bbc.co.uk/schools

Channel 4 produces schools programmes, videos and resource packs on different faiths, including 'Animated World Faiths'. C4 Schools, PO Box 100, Warwick CV34 6TZ
Tel: 01926 436444
email: sales@schools.channel4.co.uk   www.channel4.com/schools

Iskcon Educational Services, Bhaktivedanta Manor, Hilfield Lane, Aldenham, Watford, Herts WD2 8EZ
Tel: 01923 859578   email: ies@com.bbt.se
Runs programmes for schools; largest supplier of educational resources on Hinduism in Britain, with mail-order service.

The Commonwealth Institute Resource Centre Kensington High Street, London W8 6NQ
Tel: 020 7603 4535   http://www.commonwealth.org.uk